THE HUMOR
OF
MUSIC
AND
OTHER ODDITIES
IN THE ART

Compiled by Laning Humphrey

With an Introduction by
Arthur Fiedler

D1072762

CRESCENDO PUBLISHING COMPANY
Boston

715612

Standard Book Number 87597-060-5
Library of Congress Card Number 76-131050
Printed in the United States of America
Copyright © 1971 by Crescendo Publishing Company

Contents

Frontispiece by Elinor Preble, flutist with the Boston Symphony Orchestra. All others by Martha Burnham Humphrey.

Introduction by Arthur Fiedler

SOME VERY proper concertgoers severely criticised me one time, in letters to a newspaper. This was because I had conducted an uproarious parody on *The Glow Worm* on one of my annual Pops programs at the Berkshire Festival. My protesters considered that I was stimulating rowdy behavior on the part of the audience, and that my arranger had desecrated a beloved musical selection by having the glow worm burst into flames, and fire engines clanging to put them out. On the other hand, most of the 6,000 listeners kept filling the big Music Shed with bursts of laughter. For my part, I was sure that both the audience and the players enjoyed the contrast with the serious Festival music.

Contrasts are certainly vital factors in music — fast and slow, loud and soft, for example. Also the serious mood is offset by the gay — and that carries over into the life of the musician as a contrast to the serious business of concert-giving. I enjoy the unexpected, amusing experience, whether my own or someone else's. This collection of the contrasts of fun and facts in the musical world appeals to me.

Overture

"MISS X gave a recital last night. Why?" This should give Boston the permanent world's championship for the shortest and most scathing concert review. It is credited to Philip Hale, who reigned for many years as Boston's most learned and caustic critic, while reviewing music and drama for the *Herald*.

Here is just one indication of the truth that when all is said and done, the story of concert life of all kinds is the story of alternations of contention and agreement among performers, audiences, critics, and composers. As a matter of etymological fact, the ancient meaning of the verb "to concert" was this: "to contend, contest, dispute." Later, the verb came to mean "to bring to agreement; to arrange mutually." The stories in this volume will give concert life to you both ways.

LANING HUMPHREY

6

Conductors vs. Musicians
(and Choruses)

FIGHTING WITH a conductor may be hazardous to the health of a musician's career. There is, however, an interesting assortment of exceptions. The Austrian piano virtuoso, Artur Schnabel, world-famous as an interpreter of Beethoven, got away with barking at a conductor during a rehearsal:

"You are there, and I am here. But where is Beethoven?" he vociferated.

The music was resumed in Schnabel's style.

*　　*　　*

When an operatic conductor attempted to re-mold an aria as sung in rehearsal by Mattia Battistini, the great baritone applied his beautiful voice to this speech:

"Maestro, let me remind you that people buy tickets to hear me, and not to watch you. Therefore let us proceed in the way I feel this aria should be sung."

*　　*　　*

Similar assertiveness on the part of Geraldine Farrar left her the loser. When Toscanini attempted to correct her, she overrode his admonition twice, then with her grey eyes flashing, she retorted:

"You forget, maestro, that *I* am the *star*."

"I thank God I know no stars which are perfect except those in Heaven," was Toscanini's rejoinder. Farrar then followed his lead.

* * *

When a certain player rehearsed in a languid manner, Serge Koussevitzky called out to him:

"Don't play like an old man."

"You're an old man yourself," was the come-back.

"I know that," Koussevitzky replied. "BUT when I conduct like an old man, I will give up the job."

The musician went on with his playing *con spirito*.

* * *

Many of the differences which exist between conductor and musician remain on a friendly basis as evidenced by an incident which illustrates the genius of the conductor, Eugene Ormandy. During the rehearsal of a modern French work he stopped to correct the third flute player.

"You are playing F-natural instead of F-sharp," asserted Ormandy, "and you made the same error just three years ago in Chicago when we played there." The flutist was dumbfounded. Notwithstanding he immediately took issue with his director and smilingly replied, "I remember the mistake in Chicago at the concert you mention, but it wasn't in this work but rather in the Beethoven *Seventh Symphony*."

"On the contrary," insisted the maestro, "while an error *was* made in the Beethoven Symphony, the first bassoon was guilty, not you. Your error three years ago was in this French number and identical with the one made today."

The bewildered and vanquished musician conceded the victory and resumed the task of mastering his part, deciding then and there never again to differ with Ormandy.

*   *   *

Although individuals can cause a conductor problems in securing the proper response to his baton, the conflict is greatly magnified, of course, when a choral group is involved. This situation is exemplified by a plea from Beecham, addressed to one of those famous large British choruses he was rehearsing in *Messiah*. He expressed his discontent this way:

10

"When we sing, 'All we like sheep have gone astray,' might we, please, have a little more regret and a little less satisfaction?"

*   *   *

While recruiting singers in a farming area for an ambitious choral concert where tonal volume was vital, the director surveyed the sturdy figure of one candidate with curiosity, and asked:

"Can you make the welkin ring, I hope?"

"Sir," he replied staunchly, "you show me any welkin you've got, an' I'll bust it wide open!"

*   *   *

A newcomer to a large orchestra may feel that in a difficult score, unfamiliar to him, self-preservation requires that he fake the hard parts and then cue in with zest when the going is easier. Beecham's eagle eye and keen ear discovered two practitioners of this little game. To one he called out:

"It seems to be asking too much for you to be with us all the time, sir, but perhaps you would be so good as to keep in touch now and then."

*   *   *   *

Another instrumental truant caught this quip:

"You play very beautifully, my dear fellow, but do you think you might play more frequently?"

*   *   *

An American orchestra being rehearsed by Sir Adrian Boult had several different understandings of his rapid cue. His intention was to have certain instruments make a quick — and unanimous reentry after a pause. Instead, the instruments straggled into action in a sort of relay fashion. With gentlemanly regard for his being a guest of the orchestra, Sir Adrian avoided scolding the players. But, glancing in turn at the offenders, he made his point clear when he commented, "Rather a good fugue, eh?"

*   *   *

Certain particular episodes are identified from time to time with several different celebrities. Toscanini and not Koussevitzky definitely was the conductor who made a famous, unanswerable, and funny retort to an insult by a player. Toscanini in one of his well-known Italian temper tantrums had ordered the man off the stage during a rehearsal. As the player reached the exit, he shouted:

"Nuts to you!"

"It is too late to apologize," Toscanini responded hotly.

*   *   *

13

Matthew Dubourg, foremost English violinist of the 18th century, also was a notorious show-off. But he had a come-uppance in a concert conducted by Handel. On cue, Dubourg sailed into a cadenza obviously intended to impress Handel, whose powers of improvisation were renowned. Somehow the violinist got lost in his flight of fancy. After many wanderings, he concluded on the proper key.

"Welcome home, Mr. Dubourg!" was Handel's stentorian salute.

Composers In Disguise

THROUGHOUT THE musical world Fritz Kreisler built up a unique reputation for possessing an extraordinary blend of technical and interpretive powers. He enjoyed both high critical esteem and general popularity in programs that ranged widely through the great names of composers of violin music through the ages. Also, like John McCormack with his Irish songs, he introduced unpretentious compositions of his own such as *Caprice Viennois* and *Liebesfreud,* which were so charming, so artistically presented, as to captivate all elements of his hearers. Thus, the name of the living Kreisler balanced the names of the old masters printed on his programs — the 18th century's Vivaldi, Pugnani, and Padre Martini, for example.

In 1935 Kreisler confessed that the works he had attributed to the celebrities of the past had been his own compositions. Modestly assuming that the potency of his own name as a composer had its limits, he had decided to show his skill by writing in the various styles of his predecessors. The results had openly pleased his audiences and given much secret satisfaction to his ego.

*   *   *

A fellow-conspirator in misleading the public was that all-encompassing pianist, Josef Hofmann. To evade snide accusations that as a pianist he was favoring his own compositions, he showed his creativity by producing a considerable number of excellent piano pieces supposedly written by "Michel Dvorsky."

*   *   *

Although Paris critics generally had few, if any, kind words for compositions by Berlioz, they praised a *Chorus of Shepherds* in a concert conducted by him. It was announced as the composition of "Pierre Ducré, attached to the Sainte Chapelle in 1679," and performed from a manuscript discovered by the conductor in an old closet. After reading enthusiastic reviews by his customary foes, Berlioz gleefully let it be known that the pastoral was his own work. With subsequent additions it became his beautiful cantata *L'Enfance du Christ*.

*   *   *

Felix Mendelssohn was once the pseudonymn used to conceal the identity of a talented young woman composer. She, and not the famous composer, was the creator of several of the *Songs without Words* published in his name.

Credit in those instances should have been given to Fanny Cacilia Hensel, pianist wife of a noted portrait painter. She also was the slightly older (by four years) sister of Mendelssohn. He adored her, but when she told him of her ambition to become a composer, he was positively shocked. To his early 19th century way of thinking, such an activity would turn her thoughts aside from those concerned with maintaining her proper place in the world — as wife and mother. Possible public acclaim and attendant social pressures would be ruinous to Fanny's womanliness. To make her happy, Felix condescended to include some of her piano pieces in his *Songs without Words*. It would be fun to know how this stuffy brother must have reacted when Queen Victoria specified one of Fanny's compositions as one of her very favorite numbers in Felix's collection!

What's In A Name?

IT WOULD seem only reasonable for a well-established, widely admired musician to expect his name to be generally familiar to the public. Well, notable artists have run into notable surprises on that head.

Arthur Fiedler, the extremely popular, world-roving conductor of the Boston Pops, with his name on untold hundreds of recordings, frequently finds his name misspelled in newspapers from Portland, Maine to Portland, Oregon. It comes out FIELDER.

"Oh, that's probably just a reflex from a nation-wide interest that linotypers have for baseball," he chuckles. However, he once had a quite different experience with his name in the Midwest.

Short of cash on a guest-conducting engagement, he presented a personal check at a bank in Milwaukee. The teller, with the iciest of banker expressions, stared with deliberation at the check, then the conductor.

"I'm afraid I must question this signature," he said very gravely.

"But I have plenty of identification on me," Fiedler protested. "You must have seen my picture in the papers, announcing that I'm to conduct the orchestra."

"But consider my problem," the teller replied. "You see, my own name is Arthur Fiedler." With that he broke

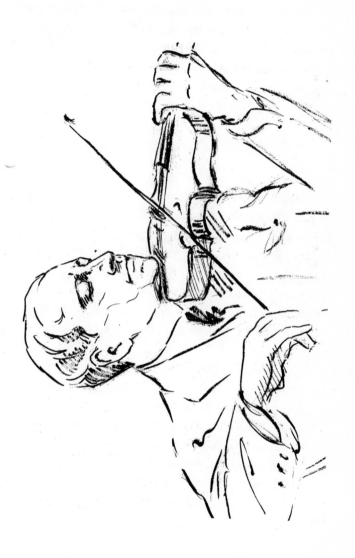

into a hearty laugh, and told the startled conductor that he was one of his devoted fans, with a large collection of his recordings. He enthusiastically accepted a guest ticket to the impending concert, and the two Arthur Fiedlers enjoyed a very agreeable snack and talk-fest afterwards.

*   *   *

One would think that any newspaper writer assigned to interview Jascha Heifetz either would have a general idea of just who was to be interviewed, or at least would make some advance preparation from the paper's reference library. But no. A girl reporter was received by Heifetz with a brief, friendly smile flitting across his customarily reserved features. After the girl sat down, there was a long silence while she fished in her handbag for pencil and paper. Then she brought the pause to a crashing conclusion.

"Now, Mr. Heifetz," she began, "How do you spell your name?"

The world-famous virtuoso slowly, distinctly, and soberly — but with a tiny ghost of a smile on a corner of his mouth — recited, as the girl nervously wrote:

"H—E—I—F—E—T—Z."

Again there was an awkward silence. The violinist ended it. With an ingratiating look and tone of voice, he said:

"Aren't you going to ask me what I do? . . . I play the fiddle."

* * *

During an interval in operatic duties, Enrico Caruso decided to make a private auto tour of some beautiful mountain scenery he had heard much about. With no previous study of the weather situation, he was overtaken by heavy rain and complete obscurity of roadways. At last he caught sight of a lighted window, and had his driver head for it. When his rapping on the door of a farmhouse was answered, he said to the man within:

"My driver and I are strangers here, and on account of the storm have lost our way to the city, and we are cold and hungry. I shall be very glad to repay you. Perhaps you have heard of me. I am Caruso."

"Come right in," the farmer said. "We're honored to be of help." Turning his head, he shouted:

"Sairey, guess who's a-callin' on us — the famous Robinson Crusoe!"

* * *

Any Russian name may have different spellings in English, French and American publications, due to several theories of re-spelling or transliterating from the Russian alphabet into the nearest pronounceable western equivalent. For

21

example, there is Tschaikowsky or Tchaikovsky; Chaliapin or Shaliapin; Prokofieff or Prokoviev.

Originally the last name of Boston's famous Russian-born conductor, Serge Koussevitzky, was transliterated as Kusevitsky. That also was the family name of two other musicians. One had the given name of Fabien. Like Serge, he became noted both as a soloist on the double-bass, and as a conductor. First names frequently being dropped from concert announcements, it became confusing to the public to know which artist was which. Since Serge was Fabien's uncle, and his senior by nineteen years, he argued his junior into adopting a change of name — as a benefit to both men. Thereafter the Kusevitsky who was to become conductor of the Indianapolis Symphony Orchestra from 1937 to 1955 was known as Fabien SEVITZKY.

The third Kusevitsky, a contemporary of the other two, bore the first name of Moshe. He was a remarkable singer, active in the double capacity of cantor and concert artist. Born in Poland, he was no family connection of Serge and Fabien. In fact, when Serge saw a poster outside Symphony Hall announcing the impending song recital there by "The World-Renowned Kusevitsky," he commented:

"So . . . but I never heard of him."

*   *   *

On arriving several hours ahead of his song recital scheduled for a city he had not previously visited, Lawrence Tibbett set out to make a purchase at the local record store. He had promised to send his recording of the Prologue to *Pagliacci* to a friend. On reaching the store he asked the clerk for the desired disk.

"There is no such recording," the clerk replied tartly, implying that this stranger was talking nonsense.

"But I know there is such a record," repied Tibbett pleasantly. "I made it."

"We have no such name as Tibbett on our list," she replied coldly.

Patiently, in an effort to be helpful, the baritone spelled the name out for her, slowly. Gradually light dawned. "Oh," said the girl, "we call that Teebay. Do you really pronounce it Tibbett?"

"Why not?" responded the amused opera singer. "I am an American, not a Frenchman."

*   *   *

A real French name has been a problem to a considerable number of Americans for a long time — that of conductor Pierre Monteux. The last name should be pronounced, of course, MOHN-TEH, with the first syllable sounding like *moan,* with the *n* smothered in a nasal sound; the last syllable should sound like the last half of *deter,* without

23

the *r*. But often the name comes out MON-TOE.

(When in his eighties, Monteux signed a twenty-five year contract as principal conductor of the London Symphony Orchestra — on condition that he could have an option for another twenty-five years!)

*   *   *

Among the individual attributes of Pierre Monteux was a modesty not characteristic of conductors. On a tour, he found that his hotel reservation had been overlooked. When the manager discovered that his disappointed would-be guest was a celebrity, he tried to explain himself out of the situation. Lamely, he said that he had not realized Mr. Monteux was *somebody,* but now, of course, a room could be assured.

"Everybody is *somebody*," the conductor declared, then turned and headed for the street.

*   *   *

Modesty among musicians makes an interesting study. As a case in point, once Jascha Heifetz and his senior professional colleague, Mischa Elman, were dining together. A bellboy presented a sealed message inscribed "To The Greatest Violinist in The World." After a quick glance, Heifetz said:

"You open it, Mischa."

"Oh, no," Mischa modestly protested. "You open it, Jascha."

Each lent a hand — or knife — to open the message.

The salutation read: "Dear Fritz."

* * *

Modesty apparently had no part in the make-up of Sir Thomas Beecham — although there is room to believe that he posed as a brash egotist for the fun of watching its effect on people.

Fritz Reiner, highly esteemed like Beecham, as orchestral and operatic conductor, was gracious enough to go back stage to meet the Englishman, who had finished conducting an opera of Mozart.

"Thank you for a delightful evening with Beecham and Mozart," Reiner said.

"Why drag in Mozart?" is Sir Thomas' reported reply.

* * *

Another example of such jocular egotism originated at a birthday dinner for Sir Thomas. Telegrams from musical celebrities everywhere were read and applauded. At the end, the honored conductor removed his cigar, assumed a facial expression of disappointment, and asked dolefully:

"What . . . nothing from Mozart?"

* * *

Among performers who have thrown modesty to the winds, perhaps the champion hurler was Vladimir de Pachmann. First he was a poet of the keyboard, with a marvelously delicate touch and suavity of tone, which made him unrivaled in the more intimate works of Chopin. Then he gave way more and more to eccentricities that earned him the nickname of "The Chopinzee." He made faces and talked to himself and his audiences while he was playing. Here is one example among hundreds:

"Bravo, bravo, Pachmann! Only Pachmann can play dis like so . . . All de greatest pianists is egotistical. Godowsky, he is egotistical, Paderewsky, he is egotistical, but Pachmann, he is de most egotistical!"

One Must Keep Up
One's Strength

SINGING AND eating seem closely associated, somehow, in regard to many opera celebrities. The explanation, according to one theory, is that great singers often have come from poor families which could afford only the plainest foods, and in limited quantity, for the children. Hence, in adulthood, a successful singer from such an origin would almost instinctively think that one function of money was to buy foods in quantity and quality denied in childhood. Another theory — originating with the singers themselves, it may be suspected — is that plenty of nourishment is required to keep up the strength necessary to maintain lung power, and hence vocal power, adequate to fill an opera house.

Caruso exemplified both theories. He loved to explore New York for good eating-places — especially those serving the best of Italian fare — and his capacity was great. However, he was astonished when he caught sight of Ernestine Schumann-Heink in a restaurant. On her plate was a huge steak. With curiosity mixed with a tingle in his palate, he said to the great German contralto:

"Stina, you are not going to eat *that* alone?"

"No, not alone," she assured him. "Mit potatoes, also vegetables, and spaghetti."

27

There is no denying that Schumann-Heink did have a powerful voice to maintain. To that end she could eat without regard to gain in weight, her operatic characters and their costumes presenting no diet problems.

*　　*　　*

A counterpart to Schumann-Heink in ampleness of voice and appetite was the Italian contralto, Marietta Alboni. Rossini was so impressed by the voice of Alboni as a young girl, that he made her his only pupil and coached her in the way he desired her to sing roles in his operas. This was invaluable for the girl. Rossini was a singer himself, and had a masterly knowledge of the art of *bel canto,* in theory and practice.

The voice of Alboni developed into an instrument of combined power and beauty, with perfect evenness over a range of two and a half octaves — from low G to soprano high C. After spectacular successes in opera and concert appearances throughout Europe, she repeated her triumphs in the principal cities of the United States in 1852-53.

Alboni, presumably to keep up her strength for her many engagements, ate heartily. As a result, she became enormously fat. Her appearance dictated retirement from opera. Yet she retained her magnificent voice. She continued active on the concert stage by singing while seated in a capacious chair.

* * *

It seems hard to believe, but at the world premiere of *La Traviata* the heart-gripping death scene of Violetta met with boisterous laughter from the Venetian audience. There was an excuse, however. The role of the heroine, wasted away by tuberculosis and about to die, was sung by Signora Salvini-Donatelli, one of the heaviest women to be seen on or off stage in Venice. This fiasco was off-set, fortunately, when the opera was repeated one year later in a different Venetian theater, with a less overfed-looking Violetta.

* * *

One unmistakable factor in the rapid success of Geraldine Farrar in Germany and her own country afterward, was her trim figure. It made her a refreshing contrast to sopranos whose personal upholstery, if somewhat excessive, was accepted traditionally as a concomitant of an exceptional voice. Gerry, incidentally, had a defense against over-eating — a nervous stomach. She had to be very careful as to what and how much she should eat.

* * *

At the outset of his career, Lablache had a generous-sized figure which was in good proportion to his great height. His voice was of such amplitude that, it is said, he could be heard with pleasure by people standing outside the opera house. With this extraordinary voice and the many engagements it attracted, Lablache supposedly had to maintain his strength by eating. At any rate, his figure expanded enormously. A popular assertion was that a baby could have been clothed in one of his gloves. But corpulence was no disadvantage to his artistic progress. It gave dignity to his serious characterizations, and conversely added hilarious effects to his comic roles.

*   *   *

Gigantic basses with voices and appetites to match seem to be born a century apart. In the mid-1600s such a singer belonged to the choir of the Elector of Saxony, with the renowned composer, Heinrich Schuetz, as Chapel Master. According to Schuetz, the voice of the bass was simply exquisite. He deplored the threatened loss of the man because of inadequate salary. Although the singer is not named in a plea in his behalf written by Schuetz, he obviously had what Rossini considered as the three greatest qualifications of a singer — voice, voice, and voice. For instance, the Chapel Master wanted him in the choir despite the fact, cheerfully admitted, that outside of his value as a singer, he was a shiftless fellow with the habit of guzzling a keg of wine a day. That also was condoned by Schuetz with an extraordinary excuse that helps us to picture this phenomenal bass. He had an exceptionally wide throat, which required more moistening than an ordinary one!

Hair

AMONG CONDUCTORS who appear to be emulating the American bald eagle is William Steinberg, music director of the symphony orchestras both of Boston and Pittsburgh. Describing a certain vexing incident of one season, he said to some friends:

"So there I was, tearing my hair."

Then he clasped his pink skull, and added:

"WHAT am I saying?"

*   *   *

Hair has been an extra dividend in the success of some artists. Frances Alda's soprano voice was expressive, but not opulent. Her luxuriant red hair supplemented her audience appeal — as she knew very well, and she made adroit use of that bounty in planning her costumes. (If the costuming of a role called for tights, one critic said she had two particular advantages added to her voice. These were her right and left legs.)

*   *   *

The dark brown, almost black tresses of Geraldine Farrar added planned emphasis to the acting ability which went with her excellent voice.

*   *   *

In the case of Maria Jeritza, the blond glory of hair and features that crowned her superb figure was both an asset and a liability. Distracted by her beauty, cynical members of her audiences professed that she was dependent on her charms as a substitute for vocal and dramatic virtues. However, she was outstanding in both respects.

*   *   *

It is to be wondered how long it would have taken Paderewski to raise an international furor as piano virtuoso without his deep halo of red-gold hair, which mightily fascinated the ladies.

Hosts of feminine idolaters wrote frenzied appeals for a lock of Paderewski's hair. The demand would really have made serious inroads on the supply. According to a concerned secretary, he thought feminine devotion was too valuable to be discouraged. Despite the extent of the requests, he took care of them — after a fashion. He bought a dog whose hair was a close match for Paderewski's and went to work with scissors.

A similar story is told of an earlier musical hero adored by women. This was the Waltz King, Johann Strauss, Jr. Was his example followed in behalf of the pianist, or was it independent thinking?

Tricks — No Treats

EVERY so often, unknown to audiences, supposedly serious artists of the stage play tricks on each other. Such acts are sometimes reprehensible and often funny. Their excuse is the struggle between art and the boredom of constant repetition of the same scenes. Certainly they are dangerous tests of nerves, which also serve as subjects for after-performance conversation or recrimination, and ultimately legends.

Caruso, in the midst of a soprano's aria, peered intently at her wide-open mouth and whispered:

"How would you like a nice, juicy steak?"

* * *

Caruso's spirit of fun was shown at least once in full view of an audience. When he and Frances Alda took a curtain call, ushers repeatedly handed up flowers for the Australian soprano. The tenor kept assuming a hopeful expression, only to register disappointment as the bouquets went to Alda. Finally he spied one waiting to be delivered. All anticipation, he grasped the flowers himself and eagerly sought out the card of presentation. Reading it, he showed no joy, and glanced glumly at the audience and Alda. She quickly presented a rose to Caruso, who broke out into a characteristic broad smile. The pair made a happy exit to the accompaniment of laughter from the audience.

*   *   *

Caruso is also accused of having pressed a warm potato into the chilled hands of Mimi in *La Boheme*.

*   *   *

Poor Mimi's cold hands were surreptitiously warmed again, in a small Italian opera house. The American tenor, Frederick Jagel, in the role of Rodolfo, the lover, decided after many performances to do something about those hands. In the muff given by kindly Musetta to Mimi he secreted a warm sausage.

*   *   *

An example of slipping a surprise into a performer's hand occurred while the original dramatic version of *Pelleas et Melisande* was being staged in London. Sarah Bernhard, who liked to take male roles, played the hero, and Mrs. Patrick Campbell the unhappy heroine. At one point, where Pelleas was to take Melisande by the hand, Sarah crushed an egg within it.

*　　　*　　　*

In the title role of Boito's *Mefistofele* the great Russian bass, Feodor Chaliapin, found inspiration for one of his most impressive feats of singing and acting. Nothing more magnificently sinister could be imagined. On the other hand, he had a rather light-hearted attitude toward the Devil of Gounod's *Faust*. He was as likely as not to introduce some gay improvisation in this role, during an actual performance. One instance took place during the country fair scene. It calls for the presence of Marguerite's would-be young lover, Siebel, a role that by convention is taken by a mezzo-soprano as likely-looking as possible. On the occasion in question, Chaliapin, looking down from his height of six feet five or so, was amused at the diminutiveness of Siebel. During the waltz episode in the fair, he stooped, whisked her up clear of the stage, and waltzed around with her feet in frantic motion, and her body squirming, in an effort to be set down. It certainly was good for laughs on the part of the audience.

*　　　*　　　*

Chaliapin was in a class by himself in this century, with

37

his towering and sturdy figure, combined with the munificence of his voice and his prodigious art as an actor. Historically he had a rival in the preceding century. This singing actor was the half Irish, half French bass, Luigi Lablache. He was another gigantic figure of a man. Like the Russian, he also aroused debate as to whether he was greater as singer or as actor. Again like Chaliapin, who could be dramatically stunning as Czar Boris, or uproariously funny as Don Basilio or Leporello, Leblache was a master of the dramatic and the comic role interchangeably. As for his physical prowess as compared with Chaliapin, consider this. In the role of Leporello he would pick up the full-grown man singing the part of Masetto, and carry him off stage tucked under one arm.

Quick Thinking To The Rescue

OVER AND above painstaking preparation for a performance, quick thinking can be a valuable asset to a performer
or conductor.

While Charles Munch was directing a New York performance of Berlioz's *The Damnation of Faust,* the tenor
suddenly whispered that he was too ill to go on with his
forthcoming important solo — and he quickly left the
stage. Just as quickly, Munch mouthed the word "Cut!"
to the orchestra, gave the players the phrase where they
were to come in, and signalled the baritone, Martial
Singher, that he was to sing his part then, instead of later.
There was no break in the concert. Since cuts are often a
matter of advance planning in long works, most of the
audience seemed undisturbed, although perhaps a little
surprised at the departure of the tenor.

*   *   *

In a famous love scene in Leoncavallo's *Zaza,* Geraldine
Farrar in the name role was baffled when Martinelli, as
her lover, sat down on a sofa instead of embracing her.
Improvising, Gerry leaned over the back of the sofa and
whispered "Are you ill?"

"No — my suspenders let go," Giovanni replied with

39

a worried look.

Gerry did her best to save the scene by leaning flirtatiously on the sofa-back, trying to make it look like a response to Martinelli's love-making. What else could she do? But the critics accused her of trying to "hog the scene," which belonged to the tenor.

*   *   *

Not only singers themselves, but their voices, are subject to vagaries of temperament. Under nervous tension, a singer may open his or her mouth without any sound emerging. This happened to the bass, Andres de Seguerola during the last act of *La Boheme*. He got set for his great solo, *The Coat Song,* attempted to flex his voice under cover of the orchestra, then turned a terrified gaze to Caruso, pantomiming "No voice!"

"Make the words with your lips — I will sing for you from in back," Caruso whispered. From taking part in many performances, he knew the solo well and using a dark shade of his big voice, he gave a good imitation of a bass-baritone rendition.

*   *   *

"I remember," John McCormack told some friends, "when I was making my debut in opera as a mere boy in Turin.

I had to take an upper C. I knew how accustomed these Italians were to robust high notes, so I determined not to let them down. I told the orchestra conductor to give me a chance when the note came along. And sure enough, he subdued the orchestra somewhat and I rang out the note.

"I really felt I had made a pretty good job of it," observes the Irish tenor, "but not a hand clapped!

"The following night I told the conductor when coming to this passage again to let his orchestra go in all its power and volume. He did. The volume filled the theatre. The rafters shook. And I flung my head back and opened my mouth wide and made a face of tremendous effort — but actually not a sound did I let pass my lips. I thought the roof would come off with the thunder of applause! All for a note I had not even begun to utter!"

*   *   *

Sametini was playing in Marion, Indiana, and had forgotten the suspenders for his evening trousers. "With no belt loops the use of my belt was out of the question," he remembers. "It was late. Shops were closed. I was not sufficiently resourceful to improvise a makeshift pair of braces and hence it was with some anxiety that I left my room to walk to the scene of my concert that night.

"On the way I chanced to meet a laborer on the street and immediately I had a divine inspiration. Solely for the purpose of starting conversation, I inquired as to the location of the church in which I was to play. Then I casually mentioned the fact that I envied him. He looked surprised. 'Why?' he inquired. "Because you wear suspenders," I replied in all seriousness. Now an interested listener, I told him of my plight. Promptly and without any reluctance, he took off his braces and handed them to me, adding, "I'll stick around till the concert is over; I love music."

*   *   *

Beauty of voice in a tenor is not too often combined with a gift for dramatic action. Tito Schipa however, has been credited with a flash of drama that contributed to his success as the hopeless lover in the name role of Massenet's opera *Werther*. Actually, a stagehand was a silent partner in the special dramatic stroke. The scene involved showed Werther re-visiting his beloved Charlotte after a fruitless effort to forget her. During rehearsal the door produced a silly effect by popping open each time Schipa closed it. The stage director ordered a stage hand to secure it during the performance, after Schipa made his entrance.

But plans went askew in the performance. As Schipa passed through the door, it was closed firmly on the pigtail of his 18th century wig. It was clear to him that if he

took a single step forward, the wig would come off and comedy would result. As if by dramatic motivation he stood there as gracefully as he could, singing tenderly to Charlotte half a stage away, creating the illusion of seeing her in the misty distances of a dream. The effect was tremendous. It doubtless puzzled Charlotte, but the audience responded with torrents of applause. Taking instant advantage, Schipa signaled for the door to be loosened, freed his wig and took his bows.

*　　*　　*

Early in his career Robert Merrill was thrilled at the prospect of appearing in *I Pagliacci* with Giovanni Martinelli. True, it was to be a "quickie" production in Worcester, Mass. But he would be willing to sing that delight of baritones, the Prologue, any time and under any condition. For this particular occasion he counted on earning an acceptable fee without "breaking his neck" for it. But he was wrong.

In accord with the familiar stage business for his enactment of Tonio the clown, Merrill stepped from behind the curtain to stand before the audience and introduce the play. There was nothing to stand on, for the curtain was flush with the edge of the orchestra pit. Merrill made a frantic successful grab for the curtain and swung himself up and in to a bit of standing space. He says he nearly broke his neck in the scramble. Moreover, he was terribly embarrassed, for the audience was laughing at him without stint. He felt better on learning that they were crediting him with deliberate clowning, for he certainly was dressed in a clown costume.

44

More Than One Talent

IT IS often supposed that great musicians are such because they devote their lives to concentrating on one great talent with which they were born. This is true to such a degree that the exceptions make a fascinating study.

At the Cleveland Center of the National Aeronautics and Space Administration a man named Burton Fine put in nine years as a research chemist. He was the author of eighteen scientific papers on subjects which included chemical kinetics and thermodynamics. Since 1964 he has been principal viola of the Boston Symphony Orchestra. The fact is, that he had been trained as a violinist at the Curtis Institute in his native Philadelphia before studying chemistry at the University of Pennsylvania, then gained a PhD. in that subject at the Illinois Institute of Technology. With this combination of musical and scientific training, he was able to keep up with his music by playing both violin and viola in chamber music groups as a relaxation from chemistry. Hearing of a vacancy in the Boston orchestra's string section, he applied for an audition and as a result was placed, as a newcomer, at the last stand in the second violin section. One year later, when auditions were announced for the post of principal violinist, he entered the competition and was the victor.

*   *   *

45

Mechanically gifted, Nathan Milstein when he first came to America was told the good news that his tour opened as soloist under Stokowski, with the Philadelphia Orchestra. He brushed this aside to ask if he would play in Schenectady. He wanted so much to see the General Electric plant!

*   *   *

Our noted American symphonic composer and author of an important book on orchestration, Walter Piston, is a graduate of the Massachusetts State Normal School of Art. First he intended to become an artist, and for a while was a wage-earner in the drafting department of the Boston Elevated Railway Co. But feeling a strong impulse toward music, took violin lessons with three eminent Boston teachers, and studied piano with another. As a violinist he played dinner music in restaurants and in World War I he served as a bandsman in the U.S. Navy, thereby gaining a practical knowledge of wind instruments.

*   *   *

One of the cellists of the Boston Symphony Orchestra left that position after eight seasons, went to New York and immediately made history as a star operatic baritone. His name was Giuseppe Campanari. As a member of the Hinrich Opera Company, it was his honor to sing the role of Tonio in the first American performance of *I Pagliacci,* with Gustav Hinrich conducting. He then joined the Metropolitan Opera and further distinguished himself in London with the Covent Garden Opera. The Boston Symphony Orchestra re-engaged him as baritone soloist in nine different seasons.

* * *

As a diversion, Caruso once took up the study of flute-playing, but not for long. He dropped the lessons with the decision that this was an art in which he had an abundant lack of talent.

* * *

With the uncanny understanding which Berlioz had of the individual characterstics of each instrument of the orchestra, he would presumably be able — like Richard Strauss — to perform to some degree on any of them. Actually, his playing ability in regard to the regular instruments of the orchestra was confined to the bass drum. Outside of the orchestral category, he played the flagelette "somewhat badly," it is reported, and the guitar "tolerably well." As for the piano, it was too much for him.

* * *

Stephen Foster was a skilled flutist, although he noted down his songs without dependence on his flute or — as is the case with some of our modern popular song writers — needing a piano. Once when he was invited to a party to which he suspected he had been invited only to play the flute, he remained at home and sent the flute.

*   *   *

A very able sculptor, the Russian bass, Chaliapin combined both of his artistic skills in operatic roles, accomplishing extraordinary feats in make-up. Unerringly, he was able to transform his normal features into complete incarnations of his operatic characters — the ridiculous Don Basilio of *The Barber of Seville,* the ominous *Mefistofele* of Boito's opera, the guilt-ridden Czar, *Boris Godunov*.

*   *   *

The Spanish contralto, Maria Gay, took up sculpture and violin playing before singing her way into fame in the roles of Carmen and Amneris. She apparently was undecided whether to become a sculptress or a violinist, when she was turned to a new career by the French piano virtuoso, Raoul Pugno. While touring in Spain, he heard Maria singing for the pleasure of it. He assured her that her voice was too precious to ignore, and gave her the opportunity to sing at various concerts of his. She took vocal lessons in Paris and developed rapidly as an international operatic star. But in the contentions of such a life, she continued to find peace and artistic gratification in sculpture.

*   *   *

The pure, technique-concealing art of Josef Hofmann at the piano keyboard took the spotlight from another of his accomplishments. During the time when the player-piano flourished, he toiled in his private machine shop over apparatus for humanizing the cold, mechanical touch of the foot-operated piano and was eminently successful. Subsequently he invented a device for non-electric amplification of a small or large grand piano to compensate for a pianist's lack of power, or to avoid driving a piano too hard in a large hall. His ingenious invention, a hollow piano cover designed like a sounding board, could be substituted for any standard cover which merely kept off the dust.

*   *   *

At the age of ten a Polish girl made public appearances both as pianist and as violinist. She performed in both roles for the great pianist-composer-conductor Franz Liszt. After she also had sung for him, he advised her to take up voice-training. She did — and attained worldwide fame as Marcella Sembrich, coloratura soprano. She was not only highly regarded in opera, but also in song recitals. In one of her concerts she put her versatility on display by presenting herself as pianist and violinist as well as singer.

*   *   *

It was as a violinist that Harold Bauer was known before establishing himself as the eminent English pianist. He and Fritz Kreisler enjoyed swapping places on suitable occasions — Bauer playing violin solos to Kreisler's accompaniments at the piano.

They Didn't Need Women's Lib!

THE DOMINANT position of sopranos in the realm of high operatic fees during the "Golden Age" of singers makes interesting reading.

Five thousand dollars a performance was demanded by Adelina Patti. The pretty Spaniard was worth it, too, for impresarios knew that she could fill an opera house when others failed. Her coloratura singing was a marvelous display of effortless production of beautiful tone, with an absolutely even scale from middle C to F above high C.

One of her impresarios commented that Patti held onto her voice for such a long time because she never sang more than ten times in a month. No matter what the cost, she refused to sing if she felt indisposed in the least.

In her contracts she stipulated that she was free to omit rehearsals, and that she, not the management, would select which one of the 30 operas in her repertoire to perform on any particular date.

Her manager estimated that she sang 2,590 times in 37 years (at a fee of $5,000 a performance) or 210 times more than most prima donnas could manage in 20 years.

*   *   *

The dramatic soprano voice of the Italian, Giuditta Pasta, inspired the creation of three operas, two of which are still performed. For her, Bellini wrote *La Sonnambula* and *Norma*; and Donizetti, *Anna Bolena*. She was in constant demand in London and Paris, with the result that she made a fortune thereby.

*   *   *

Jenny Lind was paid $130,000 for her tour of the United States in 1850, with P. T. Barnum as astute manager. She gave away $100,000 of this to charities in her native Sweden.

*   *   *

One of the few singers to compete successfully with Jenny Lind for fame and fortune was not another soprano, but a contralto, Marietta Alboni. However, her voice was so much a phenomenon as to enable her to sing both contralto and soprano roles. Her range was from contralto G to soprano high C. The management of London's Covent Garden theater, enthusiastic over the Italian contralto's showing against the Swedish Nightingale, decided to pay her 2,000 pounds a season. That was a whopping wage in 1847. Alboni became so wealthy as to be able to make a large bequest to the City of Paris. In appreciation, a street in the suburb of Passy was named for her.

*   *   *

During a "talk fest" centering on a Metropolitan Opera primadonna, someone asked her what opera was to be presented the following Wednesday. The haughty reply was: "I can't tell you. *I* don't sing that night."

Sportsmen Too?

PERSONALITIES OF the musical world have resorted to a variety of methods to escape from the tedium of their respective routines. Attending boxing matches was a formula for Beecham, Toscanini, (Arthur Fiedler still does) and the famous English critic, Ernest Newman. In fact, Newman showed his acquaintance with the sport in one of his concert reviews written as guest critic for the New York Evening Post in the season of 1924-25. Reporting on the second act of "Tosca" with Maria Jeritza in the title role, and Antonio Scotti as Scarpia, the Englishman wrote:

"It was the roughest *Tosca* within my experience. Never have I seen two characters mix it like this. Other Scarpias allow themselves to be counted out after the first jab of the table knife. Mr. Scotti rose at the count of eight and the uppercut with which he was at last put to sleep was a beauty.

"The winner left the ring without a mark. The weights were not given in the programme, but Madame Jeritza had the advantage in reach."

*   *   *

Physical culture was practiced as well as preached by the French baritone, Victor Maurel. He even took boxing lessons from the champion, Gentleman Jim Corbett.

*   *   *

In our times, there are prominent musicians who are practicing athletes — as distinct from the armchair types — and also a capable coach. Vienna's great conductor, Herbert von Karajan, excels as a skier. Although now in his sixties, he can give lessons in the thrilling art to his juniors.

*   *   *

Jascha Heifetz once held a championship in table tennis. This fact may have had something to do with fellow-violinist Nathan Milstein's taking up the game. Beating Heifetz in one set-to was a great thrill for Milstein. To underscore his achievement, he pointed out that he had won the game on top of the ordeal of playing Mendelssohn's Violin Concerto, with Toscanini conducting.

*   *   *

Fencing was the sport at which the opera baritone Cesare Siepi, was skilled. In fact, he was so good at it that he barely missed a place on Italy's Olympic team.

*　　*　　*

Before winning fame as a great singing actor in such roles as Don Giovanni and Boris Godunov, Ezio Pinza was a six-day cyclist.

"Incidentally, what do cyclists do," he was asked, "when they have to drop out of the sport?"

"They can open bicycle shops, as many do — or go into grand opera, as I did," he answered.

*　　*　　*

If piloting one's own airplane counts as a sport, three such sportsmen are on record among musicians. They are: Herbert von Karajan, conductor; Jose Iturbi, pianist and conductor; and Danny Kaye, singer and immensely talented guest conductor of leading symphony orchestras in the States and abroad, in fund-raising concerts for the benefit of musicians' pension institutes, among other causes. He is by turn funny in ribbing conductors' mannerisms and expert in securing orchestral responsiveness.

Animal Crackers

CONDUCTING THE Colon Opera Orchestra in an open air concert in the Centennial Park Auditorium of Buenos Aires, Arthur Fiedler encountered the oddest pair of listeners in all his career. During the music, he sensed out of the corner of one eye that some couple was moving toward the stage. The couple turned out to be a pair of llamas. They crouched down and with alert heads on their long necks, looked and listened with intense interest.

*   *   *

Playing to an enraptured mouse was the singular pleasure of Sylvia Lent, who, during a concert at a girl's college where mice are notoriously unwelcome, held the little rodent spell-bound in the magic strains of her violin.

"No sooner had I started playing," says Miss Lent, "than down the center aisle he came. Sedately he climbed upon the stage and sat perfectly still for a few minutes, apparently listening intently to my music. Then the music grew gay; he danced about happily. Now he tried his best to climb the piano leg in order to get nearer the source of those strange chords. But he found the ascent too difficult, and resumed his position near my feet. Sometimes he pranced about excitedly, sometimes he became quite pas-

57

sive, cocking his head from side to side. Once he gave his face and ears a thorough rubdown. But for the most part he sat quietly, listening, his little front paws waving rhythmically, his bright eyes twinkling merrily.

"Since I love all animals," continues Miss Lent, "this cunning little mouse held no terror for me, especially when he so obviously was the most entranced member of my audience. I found myself playing almost solely to him. The applause frightened him a little and each time it occurred, he retreated to the wings of the stage. The mouse was beside me almost constantly during the long program," concludes Miss Lent, "and I felt if I could always play to such appreciative souls, my cup of happiness would be full."

*   *   *

"This amusing incident," wrote Madame Maria Kurenko, Russian soprano, "took place when I was singing in opera during the first years of the Russian Revolution.

"It was the desire of the Soviet government to bring culture to the peasant folk — to the villages, the factory towns, the country schools.

"Hence we were obliged to sing not only in the opera houses in the principal cities but in the rural districts as well. These were exciting days. The peasant folk were baffled by this sudden attention and you can imagine their reaction to the sonnets of futuristic poets whose sophisticated verse was beyond their understanding.

"Once I was sent to sing the part of Rosina in *The Barber of Seville,* one of my favorite roles. The opera was presented in a cotton factory in a small town. As I made my appearance for my number, 'Una voce poco fa,' I was greeted by enthusiastic applause as I was well-known to these people.

"But I was barely into the number when I detected that the audience was behaving rather strangely. Finally they commenced laughing, at first quietly, then louder and louder until it deepened to a roar.

"Only my years of discipline and training prevented me from rushing from the stage at once. As the din continued, I felt I could sing no longer. The place was in a pandemonium. Try as I would to continue, I could not. In tears I ran from the stage and sobbed out my grief in the privacy of my dressing room.

"Presently, however, the manager entered softly. 'What's the matter, my child,' he inquired anxiously. Still sobbing I begged him to tell me what had happened — was there something wrong about my gown — my personal appearance? Laughing, he kissed my hands, and explained all. It seems that a cat, the pet of the workers, and her four kittens had followed me upon the stage. Stepping gingerly behind me, single file, they had surrounded me as I stood in the center of the stage. And they continued to look up at me as I sang. 'They seemed

to enjoy your singing very much,' he added, smiling sympathetically.

"Of course I laughed, too, upon hearing this explanation and with a light heart I returned to the stage to sing my favorite aria again . . . this time without interruption, to a joyous throng of enthusiastic listeners."

*　　*　　*

Laboratory rats in a University of Texas experiment were subjected to daily doses of Mozart, and another group of rats had Arnold Schoenberg as their daily fare. The rats as a total group preferred Mozart.

Warmth Of Heart
Not Unknown

DESPITE THE reputation of opera stars in general for being self-centered, and showing spitefulness toward other celebrities, examples do exist of a variety of kindly actions toward others.

When Caruso was to make his debut with the Berlin Opera, he was welcomed by Geraldine Farrar, who already was established there. The two became congenial associates, with the result that "Gerry" confided her fears for success in her own country, which was crowded with a galaxy of stars. Caruso predicted that in time Miss Farrar would find great success in her native land. One day at lunch Caruso suggested his confidence in her future achievements by stating, "Farrar fara," which means, "Farrar will succeed."

Gerry liked the originality and sound of the phrase, and adopted it for use in sealing all her letters, substituting it also on her note-paper for the family crest. It served also as a happy reminder of her friendship with Caruso.

*   *   *

At the close of World War I Gerry came to the rescue of

62

a famous American soprano who had settled in retirement in Switzerland, and now had suffered financial ruin as a result of the conflict. The singer was Minnie Hauk. At the age of 16 she had sung Juliette in the first American production of Gounod's *Romeo and Juliette.* Later she starred in the American premieres of *Carmen* and Massenet's *Manon.* These were all roles in which Gerry had won fame. Mixing action with sentiment, she initiated a fund-raising campaign for her great predecessor.

*　　*　　*

The American debut of the native New Zealander, Frances Alda, was with the Metropolitan Opera, as Gilda in *Rigoletto.* Her age was only twenty-five, but she had had four years of experience as a star in opera houses of Europe and South America. In the Met's cast, her distinguished partners were Caruso, Amato, and Louise Homer. They were so friendly as to give her precedence in taking the curtain calls at the end of the opera.

As soon as Alda was awake next morning, she had her maid bring her the newspapers. What they had to say of her were not reviews so much as attacks. She was called too untrained for New York, and declared to have no voice. A further heart-breaking comment was this:

"The young singer comes from the land of the sheep — and she bleated like one of them."

63

When the manager paid a visit to protest how greatly he differed from the critics, Alda told him hotly that she was returning to Europe on the next boat. Then the maid entered the sitting room, bearing a sumptuous basket of roses. Alda grasped for the gift card, and in a glow read this name and note:

Madame Lillian Nordica

"There never was a young singer who appeared at the Metropolitan who wasn't severely criticized on her debut. Melba, Sembrich, Farrar, myself — all of us have gone through what you are going through today. Have courage. Affectionate good wishes."

This was typical of Nordica. By then one of the great stars of the Met for 15 years, and an acclaimed performer in opera houses abroad, she never forgot that she had started out simply as Lillian Norton from Farmington, Maine. In order to win her way in the operatic world, she had accepted the advice to remodel her name into the Italian sounding form, Nordica.

Her timely thoughtfulness toward the distressed young soprano brought this tribute from Alda in recalling the episode:

"To the end of my days I shall never forget Nordica's generous gesture toward a newcomer whom she had never met, and to whom she had no particular reason for being kind. And always, if I have needed any urge to be cordial to young singers, I have had the remembrance of Nordica's roses and message, and what they meant to me on that dark morning-after."

*   *   *

64

The father of Enrico Caruso was a music-hating mechanic of Naples, who thought that his boy's constant singing was a waste of time. He turned thumbs down on paying for music lessons. At least, Enrico was encouraged by his mother, and after her death, by his step-mother. He sang in churches, at a chemical factory where he got a job, and on street corners. Finally his voice caught the earnest attention of a professional baritone, Edouard Missiano. How old was Enrico? Was he studying? No — no money for it. Missiano took the lad to his own teacher, Guglielmo Vergine, and persuaded him to give Enrico lessons without charge until he could earn by his voice after three years of instruction.

The lessons were interrupted by customary peace-time military service, during which Enrico was allowed — in fact, often urged — to intersperse soldiering with singing. After a year and a half, his stepmother influenced his brother to volunteer to take his place. Resuming his lessons, Enrico after six months started on his operatic career at the Nuovo Theater in his native city. Before very long his activities extended from Italy to Poland, Russia, Germany and England — then America, where he made his debut at the Metropolitan Opera House.

On a return to Italy, Caruso discovered that Edouard Missiano, who had set him on his way, was now broken in health, spirits, and financial resources. The tenor got him an engagement at the Met, which enabled him to be paid for filling minor roles in various operas — such as *The Girl of the Golden West,* in which he sang the role of Joe Castro. While Missiano was scheduled for a part in *La Gioconda,* he died suddenly, leaving a wife and three children in Naples. Caruso sent the baritone's body to Naples for burial. He cabled to the widow the large fee for his own part in the opera in which the man who had set him on the path to fame was fated not to appear.

Potpourri

IN THE eternal contention between critics and musicians, conductor Leonard Bernstein scored a victory during an engagement as guest conductor of the Boston Symphony Orchestra. His schedule called for conducting both in and out of Boston. Returning from an out-of-town date, he next had to rehearse in Symphony Hall for another program. Meanwhile, he heard that the out-of-town newspaper's second-string critic had written a scathing review. Bernstein got hold of a copy, which he read during intermission. As he faced the orchestra to resume rehearsing, he read the review aloud and with gusto, masterfully giving exaggerated expression to all hypercritical remarks. He sent the players into gales of laughter. He certainly pulled the sting, and there is no doubt that the musical gossip grapevine spread more admiration for Bernstein than gossip about "Ooh, what that critic printed about Lenny!"

* * *

After listening to a "grassroots" type of composition, a reviewer observed: "The title of the piece was *Potato Hill*. On hearing, it would appear that the subject was not a sweet potato."

* * *

George Bernard Shaw, who devoted five years to music criticism, once took a padded jab at Jascha Heifetz. He found the violinist's performance so perfect that he urged him to play one wrong note per concert, just to prove he was human.

*   *   *

On hearing a soprano whom he admired for purity of voice, Shaw went on to challenge her intonation. "I do not mean that she habitually sings out of tune, but she has to take conscious aim at the pitch, and some intervals never get quite on the centre of the bull's eye."

*   *   *

Shaw had studied voice but as a critic he did not spare himself as a singer, saying: "I developed an uninteresting baritone voice of no exceptional range, which I have ever since used for my private satisfaction."

*   *   *

For really devastating self-criticism on the subject of voice, here is a prime example from the American writer,

"Artemus Ward," (Charles Farrar Browne) a contemporary of Mark Twain, "As a singer I am not a success. I am saddest when I sing. So are those who hear me. They are sadder even than I am."

* * *

Audiences, no less than performers, have received barbs of criticism. Leopold Stokowski and Sir Thomas Beecham have distinguished themselves in this respect. Sir Thomas had no hesitancy in shouting to an audience either to quit talking, or to break off premature applause. Those he had castigated in an opera performance had their revenge, however. For months there was no applause under any circumstance, either in his opera or concert performances. Sir Thomas was forced to admit "You can have too much silence." At last he addressed a concert gathering in different vein.

"Ladies and gentlemen," he intoned, "let us pray."

* * *

Straggling, belated arrivals at concerts of the Philadelphia Orchestra became too much for Stokowsky. He retaliated by having his musicians straggle on stage after the customary starting time was long past.

* * *

Henry Taylor Parker, the Boston *Transcript* critic famous as merely "H.T.P.," or "Hell to Pay," delivered a beautiful jab at seat-neighbors who were talking during a symphony program.

"Those people up on the stage," he snarled, "are making so much noise I can't hear a word you're saying!"

*　　*　　*

Bruno Walter, conducting rehearsals with a new tenor, found him to be a problem. Although the fellow had a fine voice, he was slow picking up directions and persistently missed his cues.

Walter's patience was sorely tried when, after ten days of rehearsals, the tenor still could not start singing at the proper time. It was finally settled that the singer was to watch the director, who at just the right moment was to hold up a finger indicating that it was the singer's cue. So the curtain went up on the opening performance — with high hopes, if not complete confidence that the problem was solved. Came the crucial moment. Walter lifted his finger as arranged, and the flustered tenor blurted out in a voice audible for several rows, "Who, me?"

*　　*　　*

In a provincial Italian opera house *Carmen* was being rehearsed. After several puzzled glances at the baritone in the role of Escamillo, the conductor halted the music, and addressed the singer.

"I notice that in your Toreador Song a strange look comes over your face as you sing the phrase, 'And bear in mind — yes, bethink you as you fight — dark eyes on you are glancing.' Tell me, whose eyes do you think they are?"

Surprised, the baritone quavered, "The bull's eyes!"

*   *   *

Of all symbols of bad luck cherished by superstitious public performers — and the public itself — the number thirteen surely holds an outstanding position. What a welcome surprise it is, then, to find that this alleged bad omen has been the source of much good fortune.

A firm believer in the beneficent influence of the number thirteen is Boston Pops conductor Arthur Fiedler. He was the thirteenth among young men being auditioned for a scholarship at the Berlin Royal Academy — and won. There are thirteen letters in his complete name, a name that has brought him fame and fortune. His handsome home in Brookline, Mass. — a lucky purchase — has a street address containing two thirteens.

*   *   *

The number 13 has figured strangely in the lives of other famous artists, among them Kathryne Meisle, Metropolitan opera contralto. Many of the important events in her life were associated with Number 13 and usually when this supposedly unlucky number presented itself, Miss Meisle was sure to draw it. Dating back to her birth, she was given a name consisting of 13 letters. Coming to New York, Miss Meisle was surprised to find her charmed number again in evidence in the name of her vocal teacher. It was on Friday, the 13th, that the Chicago Opera Company engaged her to sing leading roles, and her debut role of Erda in *Siegfried* was assigned to her on that date. Miss Meisle's Victor contract was signed on a thirteenth, and her first record was made on February 13. And it was on Friday, the 13th, that she signed her contract to sing contralto roles with the Metropolitan Opera Association!

*   *   *

Lily Pons feels that way about the number 13, too. 13 is lucky for Lily! She even occasionally wears a 13 pin on her dress. Andre Kostelanetz, her husband, explained that he had proposed 13 times before he was accepted. He painted a whimsical picture of his courtship. "I made 13 trips to the coast and back by air," said he. "I proposed to Lily every time I went out. She wouldn't accept me until the thirteenth time." The conductor confessed she refused to fly east with him until he was making trip 13.

*   *   *

A subtle joke was gotten off by Hans von Buelow at a
concert in which he was appearing as great pianist, rather
than great conductor. At the same time he showed himself in his third famous capacity as caustic critic. The
program was not devoted entirely to him. Immediately
before his portion a woman vocalist gave a solo. She sang
quite painfully. Von Buelow then entered the stage,
bowed to the audience with great dignity, and seated himself before the keyboard. When he began playing something different from his announced opening number, part
of the audience assumed that he was warming up his
hands and testing the piano action. Other listeners showed
knowing smiles. The notes played were those of the baritone's entrance in the finale of Beethoven's *Ninth Symphony,* "O brothers, no longer these sad tones!"

*   *   *

Joseph Bentonelli observes that "in all Latin American
countries the end of the opera *Rigoletto* is cut.

"Just as soon as 'Gilda' has been stabbed by 'Sparafucile' she sings no more. This is not at all the way Verdi
wrote the opera.

"One night in Havana the 'Gilda" of our *Rigoletto*

was feeling quite ill. Just as soon as she had finished her actual singing role, she dressed and left the theatre.

"To get the size and form of a human body in 'Sparafucile's' sack, they secured a twelve-year-old boy to take the indisposed soprano's place within the sack. Then, in putting down the sack the basso inadvertently allowed the boy's head to strike the floor — and with a loud whack, too! This made the boy believe they were trying to play a trick on him. So the little fellow forthwith decided to turn the tables! Up he got and tried with all his might to shake off the string which bound him in at the top. Failing in this, he looked around and from the glow of the lights, faintly visible through his prison, he could see which direction was a safe one for him to travel.

"And travel he did! Like a participant in a sack race at a country fair, he waddled into the wings amid roars of laughter from the audience."

*   *   *

Eugene Goosens, English conductor, enjoyed a front view for some good fun when an amusing incident took place as he conducted a performance of *Goetterdaemmerung*.

"The opera," relates Goosens, "had gone without a hitch until just after the episode of Brunhilde's immolation, when she plunges, mounted on her noble steed, Grane, into the flames of Siegfried's funeral pyre.

"At this point it was customary to darken the stage for two or three seconds in order to allow for the lowering of the necessary backcloth, depicting the destruction by fire of Valhalla and its inmates. Alas, on this particular occasion during the blackout, which incidentally brings the opera to a close, an accident occurred which prevented the lowering of this backcloth. So, when the lights came up there was revealed to a surprised and amused audience only the crooked fragment of the backdrop, together with a large expanse of brick wall upon which was painted, in enormous letters, the somewhat inappropriate legend — No Smoking."

*   *   *

A likely candidate for the title of America's most immodest musician would be the late Silas Gamaliel Pratt. Although he was born in Vermont, any heritage of New England reserve disappeared during his upbringing in Chicago. After some basic musical studies in Chicago, he went to Berlin for further studies at the age of 22. After several years as a church organist in his home city, he returned to Germany, took some piano lessons with Liszt, and studied orchestration. In Berlin on the appropriate date of July 4, 1876 he conducted his *Centennial Overture*. It was inspired by the signing of the Declaration of Independence, and dedicated to General Grant, who was present when Pratt repeated it in London's Crystal Palace.

Pratt concentrated his career on composing in various forms in tribute to heroes and events of American history, but the highest praises of these works came incessantly from Pratt himself. This tactic backfired when critics failed to find the music measuring up to the merits proclaimed by the composer.

It may have been a sardonic critic who originated the story that Pratt and Wagner met, and the young American said:

"Herr Wagner, you are the Silas G. Pratt of Germany."

*   *   *

At one time vocal and instrumental soloists actually were not scolded, but admired for exploiting themselves beyond the intrinsic artistic needs of a musical work. In fact, composers from Handel to Rossini (who objected) invited their star performers to improvise long measures of musical embroidery — "cadenzas" — on certain of their themes. This custom was aimed at helping to insure audience success for the composer, due to "star" glamor. The cue for the performer to take off on a flight of musical acrobatics was a halt in the notation, and over the blank space a symbol like a horizontal parenthesis with a dot under it. (This "fermata" or pause-mark is known by many musicians as an "eyebrow.")

*   *   *

As Fritz Kreisler and a friend were walking along a New York street, they came to a fish market with a comprehensive window display facing the sidewalk. The violinist waved a friendly salute toward the rows of listless creatures with their glassy eyes and open mouths.

"That reminds me," he explained. "I have a concert tonight."

*   *   *

Sometimes tradition alone justifies a continued action in music (or drama) for which there is no other cause.

Victor Maurel, the French baritone, was the innocent originator of a supposed great tradition. One of those rarities, a singer who could act, he excelled in that capacity to the extent of winning success as an actor on the French dramatic stage. His example became an inspiration for a young American baritone. This was Lawrence Tibbett, who started his career as an actor, then became a singer who combined a fine voice with ability and intelligence as an actor.

In studying one of Maurel's roles, Tibbett learned that in one scene the Frenchman had scored a great dramatic effect by momentarily turning his back to the audience. This had become a tradition which, to Tibbett's way of thinking, needed a sensible explanation. He tracked down the origin of the so-called tradition. The earlier baritone had been troubled with phlegm clogging his throat, had turned his back to spit it out, and then quickly resumed his planned action greatly relieved.

*   *   *

Fights with the English language have had some peculiar results for foreign-born musicians, who seem to get along much better in various other idioms.

After Koussevitzky had criticized a choral group for not following his indications at a rehearsal, the leader of the men's section gave him this bitter rejoinder:

"We are doing exactly what you insisted on at yesterday's rehearsal, and now you blame us and confuse us!"

"My dear yonk friend, in the art is necessary to look alvays for a more better vay to do. I must change for the most artistical resultat. I AM NOT A AUTOMAT!"

*　　*　　*

At a birthday party in honor of Frances Alda, the Spanish bass, Andres de Segurola, rapped on the table for the attention of the covey of distinguished guests. Raising his glass of champagne as signal for a toast, he said:

"Alda, I speak on your behind."

*　　*　　*

That inveterate traveler, Arthur Fiedler, chose to spend one vacation in Yucatan. Just settled in his quarters in the town of Uxmal, he was told that the local band wished the honor of being conducted by him. He protested that he had come to get away from work, not to acquire any, and furthermore, his vacation would be shortened by the hours needed for rehearsing. He was astonished by the reply that no rehearsal would be necessary. All Mr. Fiedler had to do was to lead the concert.

"The bandsmen were Mayan Indians," the conductor said later. "They had no shoes. They even had no music. Their instruments included some strange specimens I'd never seen before. But they gave a surprisingly good performance of — can you imagine it? — Beethoven's *Egmont* Overture. They also were good in a Hungarian Dance of Brahms. This undoubtedly was the most unusual orchestra I've ever conducted anywhere in the world."

*   *   *

On arriving in this country from his native Brazil, Eleazar Carvalho (who eventually became conductor of the St. Louis Symphony Orchestra) agreed to an interview combined with a luncheon. As he and the reporter seated themselves, he explained that although his English was not to be compared with his Portuguese, Spanish, Italian, French and German, he would prefer to struggle in English without help — except when he was really beaten.

That situation finally developed. When the waiter inquired about orders for dessert, Carvalho studied the menu card and said:

"Vanilla a la mode."

The waiter looked helplessly at the reporter, who told him:

"What the gentleman wishes is vanilla ice cream, with pie under it."

*   *   *

Luella Melius told this story on her old German piano teacher, Herr Koletzki, in Appleton, Wisconsin. The benign old professor was painfully showing the twelve-year-old child how to play a simple melody.

After several minutes of arduous, though fruitless effort, the teacher wiped his perspiring brow before resuming the lesson.

Suddenly the child inquired, "What does M F mean all through the music, Professor?" In broken English, the exasperated man blurted, "You imbecile! Why, mit feeling, of course!"

*   *   *

To play on the expressive potentials of composers and the emotions of audiences, opera plots abound in scenes calling for the extinction of the life of one or more characters. Stabbings are prominent in *I Pagliacci* and *Cavalleria Rusticana*. Also, of course, Carmen meets her end that way. In addition, shootings occur, but are rarer. For instance, Eugene Onegin fatally shoots his rival in a duel.

In some productions of *The Masked Ball,* the Governor is shot. In others, he is stabbed. Jussi Bjoerling in the tenor role of the Governor was killed both ways at once by what appeared to be a dagger that could shoot. It happened this way. A new production of the opera was under way at the Metropolitan Opera House. One tradition called for the use of a 17th century pistol to dispatch Riccardo, the Governor. However, the antique weapon had several disadvantages. It might fail to fire on cue — spoiling the dramatic effect, or the flash might burn the victim's costume. One way out was to aim and trigger an unloaded pistol, and have someone backstage supply the bang on cue. This had been subject to bungling, so that in the Met's new production the pistol was to be replaced by a dagger. Somehow, there was a lag in communications from stage to backstage. At the performance, when the Governor's assailant, Renato, struck him with the dagger, a loud bang issued from backstage. Imagine the surprise of Robert Merrill as Renato, Jussi Bjoerling as the Governor — to say nothing of the audience.

85

In Seattle before a performance Heifetz was in his hotel room. He had ordered a light dinner for Mrs. Heifetz and himself but the food was left to grow cold while the violinist tried out a number of endings for his transcription of the Prelude of Debussy's *L'Enfant Prodigue*. As he was experimenting, trying first high octaves, then low octaves, unable to make up his mind which was better, the waiter who had been hovering about the table spoke up: "Pardon me, Mr. Heifetz, but may I say how nice it is to hear real music instead of jazz." Heifetz smiled and went on playing. Finally he stopped and sat down to eat. In the intervals between courses he and Mrs. Heifetz discussed the two endings, finally decided the matter. Dinner over, the violinist dressed for the concert, put on his hat and coat, and started to go out. On opening the door he saw a note lying underneath it. He opened it and read: "Dear Mr. Heifetz: the lower ending is better. Respectfully, The Waiter." Which was just what Heifetz himself had decided.

*   *   *

Speaking of noise in association with music, here is a thought from Beecham. "The English may not like music — but they absolutely *love* the noise it makes."

*   *   *

86

Of course, a clash of cymbals can be a thrillingly acceptable noise, as used by a composer to punctuate a musical effect. But the percussionist must be nicely on cue. Sir Malcolm Sargent put the matter neatly. Answering the question, what did one need to know to play the cymbals, he said, "Nothing — just *when*."

* * *

John Pennington of the London string ensemble said that at a large dinner party in their honor some bright individual spoke up and said, "Just what is a string quartet?" We were all somewhat reticent about answering. Finally I suggested: "Why not ask Mr. X?" Now Mr. X was not musical. He had just arrived from his native country, Holland, to study the canning industry. But Mr. X proved himself equal to the task. "A string quartet," he said without hesitation, "consists — or is — two violins, a viola and a cello, played by four weird individuals, and each one thinks he is saving the situation!"

* * *

The debut with the Metropolitan Opera of a Wagnerian tenor (not Melchior) aroused much anticipation because of his advance publicity from Europe. Apparently his uppermost thought was to overwhelm his American audience. He did. A critic wrote:

"The newcomer sounded like firing an Edam cheese from the mouth of a cannon."

*　　*　　*

An Italian tenor drew this remark:

"When an aria gives him a chance to hold a note, he holds it on and on, as if drawing long, luscious lengths of spaghetti before the faces of his audience."

*　　*　　*

Frederick Jagel, retired Metropolitan Opera tenor, vouches for Leo Slezak, not Lauritz Melchior, as having added a new and hilarious aside to the role of Lohengrin. In that character Slezak was supposed to be conveyed by a boat drawn by a magic swan, to be reunited with his fellow Knights of the Holy Grail. Of course, the swan is a mechanical contrivance, subject to mechanical vagaries. It swept right past the waiting tenor during one performance, without a second's delay.

"When does the next swan leave?" Slezak muttered.

*　　*　　*

Not fun, but near disaster, was involved in a production of Gounod's *Faust,* during the Garden Scene.

After Mephisto has introduced Marguerite to Faust and the two visitors have withdrawn, the smitten girl is supposed to enter her cottage. Then, at the window, she is to sing in exultation over being loved by the handsome young stranger, Faust. The soprano was dismayed to find the door resisting her frenzied efforts to enter. And for this to happen with the great love scene coming up! She dashed off stage, entered the cottage from the open rear of the scenery, barely in time to sing her reverie, "Il m'aime!" Meanwhile, she got a stage hand to free the door in anticipation of the fateful visit by Faust.

This episode raises a question beyond that of being either a stage hand's error or a wrong-headed idea of a joke. Could it have been an act of jealousy, aimed at preventing the soprano from winning a success?

*　　*　　*

The American bass, Henri Scott, was the victim of laughable stage arrangements in a European "Faust" production.

"In Italy," he recalled, "I sang a short season at the Teatro Adriano. The first opera was *Faust.* Now, the Italians are very much inclined to adhere to tradition, and especially is this true in regard to *Faust.*

"For example: they required that, since it is generally believed that Mephistopheles dwells in the infernal regions, he must, in order to respond to Faust's fervid appeal, come up from below. So, in Act I, I was obliged to make my appearance through a trapdoor, and in the last act I had to make my exit in the same way.

"One night as I stepped on the platform to sink below the stage, I inadvertently neglected to draw my sword close to my body in the process of descending with the result that when I had gotten about half way down, the protruding sword prevented further descent. It was then that a voice called out from the gallery: 'Look! Hell must be full; there is no more room even for the devil!"

* * *

Once while concertizing in California Yehudi Menuhin, boy genius of the violin, made a stirring radio address for funds toward reorganizing and making permanent the San Francisco Orchestra. He spoke in what was known as the Standard Oil Hour.

Yehudi's plea was especially to those within the State, asking each and all to contribute their dollars or their dollar to the fund. One lady, generous of heart, but evidently not quite understanding who the beneficiary was to be, wrote to Yehudi: "I enclose a dollar. I hope it will help you, the orchestra, and the Standard Oil Company."

* * *

Several particular efforts of Sir Thomas Beecham to get away from conductorial and managerial strife with musicians, critics, and public failed to bring peace. In answer to a question about his having had a vacation at an English lord's country place, he fumed:

"I spent a month down there last weekend."

* * *

A long sea voyage failed to relieve Beecham from tensions he thought he had left on land. On the way to Capetown he was trapped into conducting the ship's orchestra.

"Now, Sir Thomas, what do you think of the band?", he was asked.

"Wait until I get ashore first," he pleaded.

* * *

An effort at shipboard entrapment of the Metropolitan Opera star, Frances Alda, was neatly balked. During a visit to Australia the soprano let it become known that she had a collection of paintings, and enjoyed purchasing suitable additions. An Australian artist with more enterprise than genius decided to profit by this information. He booked passage on the same steamer on which Alda was making her return voyage. While the prima donna was enjoying her first hours of serene detachment from professional and social hurly-burly, the artist set up in a ship's lounge a comprehensive exhibit of his self-considered masterpieces. An invitation from the captain to view "an art exhibit" was accepted by Alda. But as she entered the lounge, her experienced eye took in the quality of the "art" in one all-encompassing glance.

"Good God!" she exclaimed, and walked without pause to the exit of the lounge.

* * *

Mrs. John C. Tobin, niece of the composer, Dr. Alfred G. Robyn, recalled a humorous highlight in his long career as pianist, organist, composer, and authority on Bach fugues.

Some years ago, Dr. Robyn went to the dentist to have his teeth put in order. During the sessions the forceps artist, who was somewhat of a singer in an amateur way, discovered his patient's musical proclivities. "Good," cried Doctor X, "then you can accompany me at several concerts where I am going to sing during the next fortnight." Robyn consented most obligingly and, after numerous rehearsals, assisted the dentist to real success at his appearances. Shortly after, the composer received a bill for $187.00, itemized as follows:

Examining teeth	$ 10.00
Cleaning teeth	10.00
Preparing teeth	20.00
Material for bridge work	30.00
Borings for bridge work	25.00
Bridge work	90.00
Chemicals	2.00
Total	**$187.00**

Nothing daunted, Dr. Robyn sent in his own bill, as follows:

Opening piano lid	$ 10.00
Putting music on rack	10.00
Playing on black keys	20.00
Playing on white keys	30.00
Playing sharps and flats	25.00
Accompanying	90.00
Closing piano lid	2.00
Laundry	.50
Total	**$187.50**

To this statement the musician carefully appended:
P.S. You owe me fifty cents.

Acknowledgments

STORIES CONSTANTLY circulate among musicians, but trying to find out the true source can be an obstacle course. However, I have enjoyed running it, and hope for a few smiles.

I am grateful to all those who have told me stories or who jogged half-forgotten memories, and especially to Martha Burnham Humphrey and Elinor Preble, whose illustrations grace this book.

LANING HUMPHREY